# I Should Have Written That Down

*A Book of Random Poems*

S.M. Naylar

Copyright © 2024 S.M. Naylar
All rights reserved
First Edition

Fulton Books
Meadville, PA

Published by Fulton Books 2024

ISBN 979-8-89221-098-0 (paperback)
ISBN 979-8-89221-099-7 (digital)

Printed in the United States of America

# Contents

Opening ............................................................. 1
What's New ........................................................ 2
Time .................................................................. 3
Haunted ............................................................. 4
Time-Out ........................................................... 5
My True Love .................................................... 6
The 31$^{st}$ ............................................................. 7
One .................................................................... 8
Too Long ........................................................... 9
Come One, Come None .................................. 10
No More .......................................................... 11
The Picture of Music ....................................... 12
Ghost Town ..................................................... 13
Dreams ............................................................ 14
The Storyteller ................................................ 15
Christmas ........................................................ 16
Turkey Day ...................................................... 17
Reflection ........................................................ 18
Accomplish ..................................................... 19
Hectic .............................................................. 20
Society ............................................................. 21
Read ................................................................ 22
A Wish ............................................................. 23
Revenge ........................................................... 24
I'm Done ......................................................... 25
The Unseen Foe .............................................. 26
Age ................................................................... 27
Me .................................................................... 28
Future .............................................................. 29

| | |
|---|---|
| Holiday | 30 |
| Childhood Home | 31 |
| A Bad Omen | 32 |
| Evening | 33 |
| Camping | 34 |
| Top of the World | 35 |
| Vacation | 36 |
| Depression | 37 |
| We Are Right | 38 |
| Last Day | 39 |
| The Relic | 40 |
| The Dungeon | 41 |
| It's a trap! | 42 |
| The Blank Page | 43 |
| Anchor | 44 |
| The Wreck | 45 |
| A Better World | 46 |
| The Concert | 47 |
| A Gift | 48 |
| The Interview | 49 |
| The Bad Guy | 50 |
| Fun Land | 51 |
| Big Mistake | 52 |
| The Breakup | 53 |
| The Cinema | 54 |
| The Old Ways | 55 |
| We're Done | 56 |
| Road Trip | 57 |
| Nightmare | 58 |
| But I'm Me | 59 |
| Truth | 60 |
| Music | 61 |
| Love Her | 62 |
| A Friend | 63 |
| A Sight to See | 64 |
| Time Away | 65 |
| Sanctuary | 66 |

| | |
|---|---|
| Hero | 67 |
| Good Guy | 68 |
| Wander | 69 |
| Dessert | 70 |
| The Old Man | 71 |
| The Man of the Sea | 72 |
| Valor | 73 |
| Prime Time | 74 |
| History | 75 |
| My Old Room | 76 |
| The Big Night | 77 |
| The Barker | 78 |
| Story Time | 79 |
| The Clown | 80 |
| The Empty Chair | 81 |
| We Are the Eighties | 82 |
| That Little Voice | 83 |
| Yo Ho | 84 |
| The Saloon | 85 |
| Wanted Men | 86 |
| The Veteran | 87 |
| A Special Recipe | 88 |
| The Fortune Teller | 89 |
| At the End of the Day | 90 |
| My Twin | 91 |
| Sticks and Stones | 92 |
| Oops! | 93 |
| Driving with Dad | 94 |
| The Commute | 95 |
| Summer Fun | 96 |
| Host with the Most | 97 |
| School's Out! | 98 |
| Justice? | 99 |
| Hang in There | 100 |
| She Lies | 101 |
| The End | 102 |
| Acknowledgments | 103 |

## Opening

Welcome to my first book
Thank you for deciding to take a look
I did my best to keep it clean
But some words are still obscene
I hope these words make you smile
Or at least help you relax for a little while
So once again I have to say
Thanks for buying my book today

## What's New

A table full of food breeds conversation
Despite the group or situation
Songs, stories, and your favorite store
Movies and memories of things you adore
With the right group, talking is no labor
Your words flow freely like jokes with your neighbor
When the meals over, this isn't the end
Break out the ice cream and start again

## Time

I sit and watch as it slips away
Causing ruin and decay
We run from it with all haste
Not knowing what we waste
Looking back, we laugh or cry
As it silently slips by
It can be cruel and harsh
As we're dragged by its endless march
So remember well my clever rhyme
And don't waste your precious time

## Haunted

My anxiety heightens as if sensing a hidden doom
Clouds of dust rise with each step as I cross the room
Disembodied voices fill my heart with fright
Thinking back to my friend's rumors now knowing they were right
Time seems to slow as I approach the door
With its caution tape and dried-on gore
My heart stops for in the room I see
The transparent form of a woman before me
As it cries, it extends its hand
Like any other fool, I ran
Scary things happen
And this event was the most
Never again shall I hunt ghost

## Time-Out

In this dusty corner I sit
In a room that's barely lit
A tear slowly rolls down my face
Oh, why did they leave me in this place
Clearly, they can see I'm sad
How did I know I was being bad
So I flushed a thing or two
What else is a bored kid to do
Why did Mom have to shout
Oh, why Did dad put me in time-out

## MY TRUE LOVE

At long last I see
The girl who gave her love to me
All my muscles turn to sand
As she gently takes my hand
The whole world is made a new
Know that we are two
I pray the Lord that we never part
For that would truly break my heart

# THE 31ST

A bloodred moon hangs in the sky
As forest creatures screech and cry
The air becomes cold and still
While creatures of the night impose their will
Will you run and hide?
Or will you risk your life for pride
The young and week stare in fright
For evil has awaken
This Halloween night

## One

The emptiness fills my heart
As it slowly tears me apart
The silence deafens as it fills my ears
Slowly driving me to tears
At the beach, I see people play in the sand
And couples lovingly walk up the boardwalk hand in hand
Which makes me think
Why don't people come around
What unknown flaw have they found
For what unknown wrong must I atone
Oh, why must I be alone

## TOO LONG

I hear your voice come through the phone
Wishing instantly that you were home
Telling stories from our past
How we wished they would last
Always insisting you were right
Always watching my back in a fight
Mentioning friends long since gone
Having not seen each other for so long
Before I hang up, I say you're like no other
And that I'm proud to call you brother

## COME ONE, COME NONE

The night air is cold and dry
As a faded program blows by
Dust-covered dolls missing patches of hair
With painted-on eyes that silently stare
Torn posters flap in the wind
Broken-down carousels that no longer spin
Burnt-down tents that housed such wonder
Colorful flags now torn asunder
The sun starts to set
It's the end of the day
It's time to say goodbye
To the ghost of the Midway

## No More

Enough
Enough
The last straw of patience is broken
Mistrust
Rage
By your deeds have been awoken
Hold my tongue
They don't mean what they say
They're not mean
They're not hateful
It's just done in play
Through these days I'd hoped I'd see
The person you used to be
So the truth to you I'll share
I know that you don't care
So in the end, with a tear in my eye
I'll pray for you and say goodbye

## The Picture of Music

I saw it all in a random tune
Like a sunny day or a dusty room
The images like notes dance by
Like a friend's laugh or a baby's cry
Melodies like emotions rise and fall
Painting pictures of beauty for all
So listen close as the notes do play
And see where they take you today

## Ghost Town

Fog covers the empty street
There is no sound but our falling feet
Old buildings crumble and decay
I'm sure they were grand back in their day
Here's the bank and an old saloon
With a dusty bar and moldy spittoon
Even the church is falling down
No life remains in this ghost town

## DREAMS

I wish I could paint with my mind
Oh, the things that we could find
A mighty dragon wreathed in flame
A colorful circus with a lion to tame
Cats with wings that jump up and fly
Towering castles that float in the sky
So let your mind wander
It's always okay
This art show is open
Each and every day

## The Storyteller

Come by the fire and sit a spell
Listen to the tale I tell
Outside it's wet and cod
But in here we relive the days of old
Let my words lead the way
To a distant place or a sunny day
How about a tale of magic and mystery
Or maybe you fancy a piece of our history
I've traveled to some interesting places
Seen many towns and different faces
So stick around, it gets better
Stay and listen to this old storyteller

## Christmas

There once was a season of joy and cheer
And it came in December at the end of the year
Decorations were hung on home and hearth
As the season was welcomed across the earth
But now it's all cliché
No heart involved
Just how much you pay
Even Santa's been made into a joke
Stealing happiness from the younger folk
It's our Savior's birthday too
Does that even matter to you
"I still have to work," most people say
It no longer feels like Christmas day

## Turkey Day

The scent of food fills the air
As Uncle Dave settles into his favorite chair
Children chase the cat across the floor
As Aunt Karen walks through the door
The food is ready
It's time to eat
"Kids, come in and wipe your feet"
There's yams, potatoes, and turkey too
So much food for so very few
Such warm feelings, I wish they would stay
All those great memories of Thanksgiving Day

## Reflection

Look into the mirror, what do you see
Does it show you who you want to be
Are all your hardships visible
How about all the trials that made you miserable
How about all the times life was unfair
Can that be seen on your face and hair
Although my reflection is from head to toe
There is a lot that the mirror does not show

## Accomplish

What are your hearts' deepest desire
What task must you complete before you expire
Is it some summit you must reach
Or a unique skill you wish to teach
Is it a place that you must go
Or a hidden talent that you wish to show
Is it gathering riches to earn and spend
What goal must you meet before your end

# HECTIC

Is it too much to ask
Not to be charged with every task
Answer that phone
Unlock that door
Pick up that stone
Sweep that floor
At work the requests never cease
What I wouldn't give for a moment of peace

## Society

Why is life so unfair
Does anyone even care
By our morals are our hands tied
Falling victim to their vanity and pride
By all accounts they are not right
But we are not allowed to fight
So we'll just brood as we sit on our hands
As all we stood for dies by their commands
Good times will come again if we wait
Someone will fix it before it's too late

# Read

Lift the cover and come on in
The adventure is about to begin
A shady plot to kill a king
Or an epic journey to destroy a ring
The scene is set in a haunted wood
Or a city street that looks like your neighborhood
What happens next?
Can you bear to look?
It all takes place here in the pages of this old book

## A Wish

To see you one more time
Would that be such a crime
I don't know what I'd say
Except to plead for you to stay
The first time I couldn't say goodbye
This time I would truly try
You would say you are always there
And I would say that I will always care

## Revenge

You just had to cross that line
And hurt that person that is mine
Your actions opened up that cage
Releasing a beast of seething rage
I'm not responsible for it will do
A world of pain now descends upon you
When people find you, they will cry
For now, it's time for you to die

# I'm Done

I want to go home
No longer do I want to roam
Slam the door and lock it tight
Turn on the TV and put my feet up for the night
Here I feel safe and warm
Free from the mindless swarm
After a long day in the crowd, it's good to be alone
After eight hours in their world, it's good to be home

## The Unseen Foe

Today I face a daunting foe
Whose hatred for me he will not let go
Insults fly from his mind
Hurting me at every chance he can find
I do my best to subdue his attack
But every day he knocks me back
This foe you cannot see for the person that I fight
IS ME

## AGE

What does it mean to get old
Why does it sound so heartless and cold
It's something that happens without consent
And usually said with evil content
For children it's a means of escape
For adults it's a reminder of lives not shaped
So live your life
Have fun
Be bold
For one day you too will be too old

## ME

What makes you, you?
Is it the things you do?
Can other people truly say
That you're not supposed to be that way
Minus your Mom and God
Who can really say you're being odd
Or your true love, I guess
And that friend that knows you best
But what if you don't know?
What it is that makes you so
In the end, one thing is true
Who cares what people think of you

# Future

Tomorrow is the unturned page
That fills our hearts with fear and rage
For some it's all that fills their mind
Like a puzzle for them to unwind
For others it's doubt and despair
Leaving them heartless and unable to care
Is it up to us to choose?
Or does someone else say if we win or lose
Do we truly have a say
While we go from day to day
Here's some advice to make life smoother
Don't sit around worrying about the future

## Holiday

Today is a day to remember
As we gather around the tree together
Family comes from near and far
Removing food and gifts from their car
The kids get together and start to play
Showing off the gifts they got today
Meanwhile the adults sit and talk of the past
Man, has the years gone fast
Then you see an empty chair
And remember why they aren't there
If this scene sounds familiar to you
It does to me too
For its events like this we all should witness
As our families celebrate Christmas

## Childhood Home

Through these streets I do roam
In this town I once called home
The old church where I learned to pray
The city park where I used to play
The empty lot where we rode our bikes
The mountain trails for summer hikes
All these places sing to me
That this is the place I'm meant to be
But then reality hits like stone
Because I can no longer call this place home

## A Bad Omen

Balloons and confetti fill the street
Despite a crushing defeat
The people's choice stood ready to win
But victory was stolen away again
Rage and anger filled the lands
For once again our fate is in their hands
How long can this go on
How long before people see that something's wrong

## Evening

The sun's light starts to cease
And the once busy town finds peace
Children head in as they are told
As the evening air grows cold
Windows in houses flicker by the light of the news
Work-laden parents take off their shoes
The smell of hot food fills the air
As the dog takes over Dad's favorite chair
Time seems to slow as the world loses its light
And the town is more peaceful as it slips into the night

## Camping

Coyotes howl as the moon gifts them with light
The fire crackles as tents go up for the night
The children gather as stories are told
Of outlaws and legends from days of old
Parents hold hands as they look at the stars
And children catch fireflies in mason jars
As the kids drift off to sleep
Both parents say without hesitation
We're glad we took this camping vacation

## TOP OF THE WORLD

It's 2:00 a.m., and I feel alive
Why doesn't anyone want me to drive
I only had a beer or two
I'm more sober than all three of you
I can do whatever I please
Why did you just grab for my keys?
For the last time, you little punk
I am not too fucking drunk!

## VACATION

I tire of the day to day
How I wish I could get away
To a sunny shore with lots of sand
Or an ancient castle in a distant land
A quiet place is what I need to find
Where I can relax and ease my mind
I don't want power and wealth
Just peace of mind and decent health
As I toil at my desk, I pray
To please let me go away

## Depression

Lately I've asked why
I constantly feel like I'm going to die
With every single step I take
And every moment I'm awake
My doctor says this isn't so
But I saw him a while ago
Why do I have this feeling of dread
Is it all in my head
I'm tired of this mental strife
All I want is to live my life

## We Are Right

The time for war is at hand
As the come to claim our land
Paint your face and grab your shield
Stand your ground and do not yield
Eyes go wide as they hear our cry
Knowing it's their time to die
The enemy starts to scream and yell
As we send their souls to hell
One by one they learn this night
With us you should not pick a fight

## LAST DAY

I'm tired of stressing about my job
And being called a lazy slob
From nine to five, I do my best
Granting the customer's request
I throw my vest on the floor
And shout I can't take it anymore
Here's my badge, you stupid twit
I'm going home
I fucking quit!

## The Relic

Sunlight pours in from holes in the room
Tree roots and cobwebs fill the tomb
There is your prize
It's ten pounds of gold
A religious relic a thousand years old
It's a cursed item, the locals say
Are you willing to risk your life today
If you can claim it, that will be quite a story
What weird things folks do for fortune and glory

## The Dungeon

Step on through the weathered door
See the wonders that lie in store
Ancient magic has brought you here
Are you brave enough to face your fear
A wondrous adventure lies ahead
In places where no light is shed

I know that look on your face
Should I go into this place

There're only riches beyond measure
Enough to fulfill your every pleasure

So will you trust in fate
Or will you run away before it's too late

## It's a Trap!

They left me here
What have I done
Fences everywhere, with nowhere to run
Strangers with name tags say it's okay
Those kids are happy, go join them and play
A loud bell rings and kids start to scatter
No one will tell me what is the matter
In a small room they tuck us away
Is this where I spend the rest of the day?
With textbooks and quizzes, none of this is cool
I do not like this place called school

## The Blank Page

I sit at my desk holding my pen
Hoping to be inspired again
Waiting for words to paint the scene
As I slowly drown in caffeine
The blank page taunts me like a child in school
Friends stare at me as I scream at the inanimate tool
Writer's block is terribly loathsome
Oh, why can't I finish this stupid poem

## ANCHOR

They call him the human chain
Keeping us in stress and pain
All you do is complain and cry
Constantly wishing you would die
But only when it's just us
When someone's here, you don't fuss
You tell the doctor that you're fine
But the moment you're home, you start to whine
You really don't care, and it starts to show
Why don't you just let us go

## The Wreck

A rust-covered bell that no longer rings
A shattered music box that no longer sings
An old life preserver still tied to the wall
Faded building blocks and a slime-covered ball
Locked state rooms that hide unknown treasure
From guests long ago that traveled for pleasure
In the lower levels, the water's up to our hip
Who knows what we will find in this old sunken ship

## A Better World

What if magic spells were real?
How would that make you feel?
Ancient knowledge taught long ago
Now forbidden because they say so
What wonders could we achieve
If all you had to do is believe
Imagine a world without limit
Imagine a world with magic still in it

## The Concert

Ease out of my room, I hope they don't see
Down to the front door and I will be free
Creep down the stairs, I can't make a sound
I hope that the dog isn't around
Crawl past the couch as they watch TV
Did they really think that they could stop me
Tonight is the concert they said I can't go
But that's not going to stop me from seeing the show

## A GIFT

Know it know in your heart to be true
That these wings are now a part of you
Gifted by God's love
So you can soar in the clouds above
Hardened scales will cover your skin
To protect the noble heart within
And from your mouth a searing fire
To conquer evil's dark desire
Your humanity has gone away
And a new dragon has been born today

## The Interview

Dress shirt and pants, notebook and pen
My interview is about to begin
Look engaged but try not to stare
As I sit in this uncomfortable chair
The last interviewer exits
She starts to cry
They call my name as I straighten my tie
Stand up straight and don't be a slob
Act professional and you'll get the job

## THE BAD GUY

Did you think I wouldn't see
The trail of clues you left for me
Spreading all those untrue lies
I hope you have said your goodbyes
We've gone beyond calling the cops
This is where your evil stops
My future is ruined beyond repair
Not that you even care
My revenge will be sweeter than honey
No, you will not be saved by your money
This situation you cannot mend
It's time for you to meet your end

## Fun Land

Upbeat music starts to play
You buy the ticket, and you're on your way
Color shops with flickering lights
Snapping pictures as you take in the sights
Roller coasters that make you scream
Vendors selling popcorn and ice cream
People in costumes from your favorite cartoon
Can I do everything in one afternoon?
You collapse on a bench as it starts to get dark
What fun you've had at the old theme park

## Big Mistake

Two men face off as it starts to rain
Both intent on causing the other pain
A shocking blow to the chin
Causes your little world to spin
You answer with a thunderous right
Hoping to quickly end the fight
Your strike inflicts a serious injury
He falls to the ground, sealing your victory
You spit on him as you walk away
Mess with me and that's the price you pay

## The Breakup

With me I wish you'd share
Why you no longer care
I gave to you my heart
Which you completely tore apart
You laugh as I cry
You're already with another guy
I guess my love was not enough
Compared to his money and fancy stuff
You both laugh as you walk away
I hope this happens to you one day

## The Cinema

The smell of popcorn fills the air
While my excitement grows as I look for a chair
Candy melts that's stuck to the screen
A kid cries because he drops his ice cream
The lights dim, causing a riot
As the adults yell for us to be quiet
The show starts, sending shock waves through me
I'm glad that I came to see this movie

## The Old Ways

This country has lost its heart
And it's slowly tearing itself apart
There once was motivation to help us fight
And morals that showed us wrong from right
With imagination to help us dream
And patriotism to drive the team
An education to show the way
For a decent job with decent pay
It's these traits that made us great
Let's bring them back before it's too late

## WE'RE DONE

What are you doing here
I thought that I made it crystal clear
That we don't want to see your face
So please don't occupy our space
Take your things and go away
Or there will be a price to pay
I've told you once before
That we aren't friends anymore
The two of us no longer mix
This friendship you cannot fix

## Road Trip

A car full of friends and pleasant conversation
As we head down the road to a new destination
A forgotten hotel full of ghost
Or a themed restaurant down by the coast
A distant town where family once stayed
Or a famous stadium where our favorite team played
Across the country to an old friend's wedding
With cheap hotels that have terrible bedding
Into the trunk our bags we will load
Say our goodbyes and head out on the road

## Nightmare

Your heart starts to race
As sweat pours down your face
A stillness drifts across the air
As you tell yourself there's nothing there
Suddenly sight and sound are heightened
And people can clearly tell you're frightened
The boisterous crowd goes quiet
As the creature appears, they cannot deny it
Your situation has been made clear
For now, they see the thing you fear

# But I'm Me

Why do people shift the blame
Do they think it's a silly game
"It wasn't me, it was you"
"What was I supposed to do"
"Why won't you do my job"
"I'm not being a lazy slob"
Their entitlement they do not hide
As they walk with a snobbish pride
Meanwhile we pick up the slack
Keeping the daily work on track
Unfortunately, they're everywhere
Affecting all of those who care
Just show up and do your best
And ignore the entitled pest

## TRUTH

Life is no dream
It mostly makes you scream
If it's not one thing, it's another
Leaving no time for you to recover
I know this isn't always so
But it's usually the way it will go
Stress will always fill your day
With family thoughts and bills to pay
It all starts when school days end
And adult responsibilities begin
As you face the pain and strife
Just remember such is life

## MUSIC

I heard a song today
That took my pain away
I escaped the daily grind
And found a way to ease my mind
Everyone has a song
That helps them get along
There's a song for every emotion
Life is the pain, and music's the lotion
In its tones you will drift
As you listen to man's greatest gift

## LOVE HER

I remember you
And the fun things we used to do
I can see the smile on your face
And feel the warmth of your embrace
We would dance till the sun went down
And walked the streets of our hometown
We watched old movies that made you scream
As we shared popcorn and ice cream
I thought those times would last forever
And that we would always be together
Then sickness took you away
Making me miss more each day
This one point I can't exhaust
I miss the love that I have lost.

## A Friend

You are not alone, he said
As he sat next to my bed
I know that you're filled with fear
But know that I am always here
Nothing is too big for me
Take my hand and you will see
My love for you will never waver
Have faith in your Lord and Savior

## A Sight to See

The stars come out to play
As the sun goes away
With no lights to hide their brightness
It is a sight that has no likeness
The moon and clouds play their part
Creating memories that touch the heart
When it comes to scenery, there are no greater
Than the artist known as Mother Nature

## Time Away

As I sit in the sand
With my cousin close at hand
With nothing but wind and sky
And the occasional car that passes by
There is nothing to tax my brain
And remind me of work's daily pain
For once my anxiety can cease
And I can finally sit in peace

## SANCTUARY

Welcome, weary stranger
Know that you are not in danger
Stow your gear and come inside
This is the perfect place to hide
Evil cannot breach our walls
You're safe with in our halls
So heal your wounds and get some rest
Before continuing your quest
In this fight, you're not alone
We will see that you get home

# Hero

Innocents are in danger, be their shield
Let evil tremble as you cross the field
Let those who murder and rape
Know that there is no escape
Evil will attack
You can take it
Fear not, little one
We can make it
Let justice guide your hand
As you drive them from this land
You will fight through blood and sweat
Until they are free from evil's threat

## Good Guy

What does it mean to be good
Is it doing what we should
And who's to say what that is
Is it what the Good Book says
But isn't that a point of view
How do we know if it's true
Is it following the law
Or does that have a moral flaw
In this argument, we can't budge
Because in the end, who are we to judge

## WANDER

There is something that calls me away
Where to, I cannot say
I've been in one place for too long
Where I feel I don't belong
My heart's desire I will follow
To a place where I don't feel hollow
Mabey the road will teach me a lesson
That will cure me of my travel obsession
What truth will I find out on the road
What revelation will I be showed

## Dessert

It's always good to be seen
It only costs a little green
Parents use it as a bribe
Especially for kids under five
In a cup or on a cone
You want one for your very own
On a hot day, it beats the rest
You know that ice cream is the best

## The Old Man

Young man, I must say
It's best if you just walk away
I'm not in the mood for your sass
And you don't want me to kick your ass
'Cause being old is a point of view
And I have faced worse people than you
You may be younger and stronger
But I'm smarter and darker
There are bad things in life of which I'm one
Get stepping, child, or your life is done

## The Man of the Sea

He looks at the sea, where he did roam
Pretending that his shipmates will come home
Seagulls taunt him with their cry
As they carelessly float by
Day by day, there he stands
Cursing his old and weathered hands
Why couldn't he go along
His back is weak, but his mind is strong
He has sailed these seas before
He could have brought them back to shore
The sun is setting as he shakes his head
If he had gone, they wouldn't be dead

## Valor

Would you like to be called brave
As they take you to your grave
Would you do what's right
When it's time to join the fight
Is patriotism a dying view
How much is liberty worth to you
Will those stars and stripes still shine
When you're called to hold the line
So I'm sorry for saying this bluntly
But are you willing to die for your country

## Prime Time

Do you think it's true
The stuff the news is telling you
The cost of living is through the roof
We know who's to blame but lack the proof
They show death and destruction from across the sea
What's that got to do with me
We got our own problems at our border
When are they going to get that in order
Train wrecks dumping toxic waste
Presidential hopefuls slandered and disgraced
The lie to us for great reviews
So why do we watch the news?

## History

History is being changed
By sad little people who are deranged
When confronted with the facts
It usually stops them in their tracks
But sometimes they double down
Making them look more like a clown
If you have real facts and not hatred
Then present them to be debated
If not, spare us your lies
With your crazy rhetoric and childish cries
The best way to fix this situation
Is good old-fashioned education

## My Old Room

The hinges creek as you open the door
While a thick layer of dust covers the floor
There are pictures and posters of heroes of old
They conjure up memories of stories once told
A model train set that's powered by steam
To drive one day was your favorite dream
Old church clothes you hated to wear
And a hand-drawn picture from sister to show you they care
The feeling's nostalgic and makes you smile
It makes you feel like a child for a little while

## The Big Night

Dress shirt, tie, and flower
I said I would pick her up in an hour
Had a shower and a shave
Promised Mom that I would behave
Borrowed Dad's dress shoes and cologne
It's my first date without a chaperone
Look in the mirror
Everything is alright
I'm totally ready for the prom tonight

## The Barker

Welcome, folks, the show's about to begin
Once that curtain goes up, you'll never be the same again
Witness death-defying feats from across the globe
And a collection of nature's oddities truly disturbing to behold
As the evening progresses, your anxiety will grow
But don't worry, folks, it's all part of the show

## Story Time

Gather round, children, it's time to hear
Your favorite story that we all hold dear
"I know that story," said Johnny with glee
"My grandmother always reads it to me"
It's about the hero and his mighty steed
Wandering the country, helping those in need
His victories are many, and it's all true
Do I look like I would lie to you
So listen to the tales of his glory
Come and hear his life story

## The Clown

I put a smile on your face
Though for me, it's out of place
There's a darkness in me I can't shake
It follows me every moment I'm awake
The doctors say it's not real
And that it doesn't matter what I feel
Even though I feel down
I'll try my best to remove that frown
So on this clown's behalf
I really hope I can make you laugh

## The Empty Chair

Smoke rings form as I sit outside
Enjoying my pipe while I try to hide
Across from me an empty chair
Wishing that my dad was there
I'd tell him how the world's evolved
And all the problems he could've solved
As my pipe loses its light
I convince myself that I'm alright
Before I go in, I stop and stare
And say good night to the empty chair

## We Are the Eighties

Hello, gentlemen and ladies
Let us talk about the eighties
When everyone was kind
And if you rented it, rewind
Phones were stuck in a wall with a cord
And micromachines were the thing to hoard
Saturday mornings were for cartoons
With cereal and light-up spoons
When car windows still moved with a crank
And if kids messed up, we got a spank
We weren't wrapped in plastic when we played
I'm glad I grew up in that decade

## That Little Voice

I need you to come with me
To go to the place you are meant to be
Leave your fears and cares behind
Your wildest dreams we're off to find
I know your current life is a waste
With unrealistic goals that you've hopelessly chased
But deep down you've heard my call
And know exactly where your feet should fall
So listen to me, I'm always in season
It's okay to trust your voice of reason

## YO HO

From sea to shore
We shall explore
Looking for unclaimed treasure
From farm to town
We'll hunt you down
For killing is our pleasure
With rum and gun
We'll have some fun
Causing a bloody riot
We follow no law
And it's freedom for all
When you live the life of a pirate

# The Saloon

The wooden door swings in the breeze
As the piano player tickles the ivory keys
The clicking of chips help keeps the pace
As the players all hide their best poker face
The hero enters with his guns and white hat
Asking the barkeep where his rival is at
The rival turns as he slams down his drink
But the hero draws and fires before he can think
The barkeep sighs. "It must be high noon"
This regularly happens in this old saloon

## Wanted Men

They nail a wanted poster to the wall
It doesn't look like me at all
My footsteps echo on the cobblestone street
As I duck into the pub where my crew said we'd meet
The ale flows freely as we plan the big score
Barmaids and patrons scatter as soldiers crash through the door
With our pistols drawn, we prepare to fight
I down my ale for this could be my last night

## The Veteran

An elderly man on a bench started to cry
When a teenager stopped and asked him why
He said because there were terrible things he had to view
"When I was about as old as you
And back then I had lots of friends
Most of whom met horrible ends
So sometimes when I sit alone
I think of those who did not come home
Remember that your freedoms came with a cost
It was the lives of the friends that I have lost"

## A Special Recipe

In the kitchen I do sneak
Opening the door with a quiet creak
The three of them laugh as they mix their brew
I crawl under the table for a better view
A strange odor whiffs up from the pot
Its potency increases as it gets hot
Mom turns on the light and asks what I am doing
I'm just trying to see what my aunts are cooking

## The Fortune Teller

Step into the circle and clear your mind
The wonders of your past we hope to find
Faded pictures and a scribbled name
Memories of relatives with forgotten fame
I'll light these candles to help the spell
And we'll see what stories your past can tell
I'm losing the vision, it's starting to fade
That's the best I can do for what you have paid

## AT THE END OF THE DAY

I feel myself mentally drained
I work all day with nothing gained
Minus food for another day
My goals haven't been accomplished in any way
It's been like this for a couple of years
Trying to look successful in front of my peers
How much sacrifice is enough
For us to get the finer stuff
Or just enough to feel content
While making enough for food and rent
Can someone please tell me why
It's so hard to do more than just get by

## My Twin

What are you doing over there
Don't just sit around and stare
I can't hear you, but I can see
You're supposed to be here with me
What do you mean you can't pass
There's nothing between us but glass
Don't worry, my twin, for I'm getting nearer
To finding a way to free you from that mirror

## Sticks and Stones

Rise above the words they say
Let your resolve be the price they pay
Their opinions don't pave your path
So spare them your unholy wrath
Know that you are the captain of your ship
Don't let their words ruin your trip
Show them you are of higher stature
And that in the end they don't matter

## Oops!

Going to tie Velcro shoes
Grabbing keys you no longer use
Looking for sunglasses that are on your head
Not taking off your shoes before getting in bed
Trying to push a door that says pull
Putting ice in a cup that's too full
Although they laugh, your friends offer condolence
For we have all suffered from life's little moments

## DRIVING WITH DAD

Dad and I get in the car
I hope the place is not too far
I promised him that I won't be naughty
And that yes, I have gone to the potty
He turns up the radio for our favorite song
And my car seat rocks as we sing along
I hold on to my drink with an iron grip
'Cause Dad said no spills on this road trip

## The Commute

I just had to leave work at five
Now I'm stuck in the evening drive
The cars are moving like a drunken snail
I blame my boss for this scheduling fail
This idiot is on his phone
And this lady is in the diamond lane alone
Why can't folks just use their brain
As the traffic slowly drives me insane

## Summer Fun

The smell of sunblock fills the air
As brother grabs the blanket and chair
Tightly I hold Mom's hand
As Dad drags the cooler through the sand
Lunch and sandcastle building starts the day
As brother chases the seagulls away
"You can go in the water," the fun is in reach
That's what I remember when we went to the beach

## HOST WITH THE MOST

It's been ages since I've had guest
Hopefully I look my best
Forgive the lack of light
The house must be a frightful sight
I'm sorry the stairs still creek
Ishmael said they were fixed last week
Here they come
What's their scheme?
How dare they look at me and scream
I happen to be a decent host
Despite the fact that I'm a ghost

## SCHOOL'S OUT!

No more dirty looks from teachers
No more getting beat up behind the bleachers
No more cafeteria and its disgusting food
No more notes to parents for being rude
No more laps from coaches past their prime
No more rushing to classes to get there on time
No more ridiculous clothing just to look cool
No more time wasted in this fucking school

## JUSTICE?

Why is there any debate
When it comes to choosing one's own fate
Who besides you have the right
To say when to run or fight
There are some who give no choice at all
They demand that you take the fall
There's no exception to their rule
To them you are no more than a tool
Right or wrong doesn't matter
Just as long as they get fatter
The don't care who they condemn
Just as long as it's not them

## Hang in There

Know that not all is lost
And you must go on at any cost
There is always another way
To fix the thing that ruined your day
Bad things don't last forever
We'll find a way around it together
When you're at the end of your rope
Always know that there is hope
And that no matter how bad the sorrow
There is always a fresh start tomorrow

## She Lies

Why has it come to this
Surely this wrong you can dismiss
I did not mean to cause you harm
I only meant to raise alarm
I didn't betray you
You know me better
Why else did I send that letter
She only wishes to take us apart
By claiming I tried to steal her heart
So I only have one thing to ask
Did she send you on this task
Why must we fight one another
Please don't make me hurt you, brother

## The End

Oh my god, what is that sound
A tolling bell that shakes the ground
The air grows cold and still
As a shadowy figure moves in for the kill
Tears fill a young girl's eyes
As she quietly meets her demise
But do not show this creature hate
For it was time for her to meet her fate
And we too will breathe our last breath
When we cross paths with the angel of death

# Acknowledgments

To
Robert Knight
Cameron Desrosiers
Michael Jenison
Alex Martinez
Jennifer and Ryan Reid
Sean and Debbie Naylar
Jos Taylor

Thanks for hearing these before I printed them.

## About the Author

Born in Arcadia, CA, in August of 1981
Grew up in Sierra Madre, CA
Went to and graduated from Pasadena High School
Loves anything medieval
Loves a good joke